THE LITTLE BOOK OF
EASTER

First published in 2026 by OH
An Imprint of HEADLINE PUBLISHING GROUP LIMITED

1

Disclaimer:

All trademarks, copyright, quotations, company names, registered names, products, characters, logos and catchphrases used or cited in this book are the property of their respective owners.

Cataloguing in Publication Data is available from the British Library

ISBN 978-1-03543-650-7

Compiled and written by Malcolm Croft
Editorial: Phoebe Hills
Designed and typeset in Avenir by Tony Seddon
Project manager: Russell Porter
Production: Arlene Lestrade
Printed and bound in Dubai

Headline's policy is to use papers that are natural, renewable and recyclable products and made from wood grown in well-managed forests and other controlled sources. The logging and manufacturing processes are expected to conform to the environmental regulations of the country of origin.

HEADLINE PUBLISHING GROUP LIMITED
An Hachette UK Company
Carmelite House, 50 Victoria Embankment, London EC4Y 0DZ

The authorised representative in the EEA is Hachette Ireland, 8 Castlecourt Centre, Dublin 15, D15 XTP3, Ireland (email: info@hbgi.ie)

www.headline.co.uk www.hachette.co.uk

THE LITTLE BOOK OF Easter

A CELEBRATION OF LIFE, LOVE AND JOY

CONTENTS

INTRODUCTION

It's Easter! About bloomin' time!

'Tis is the season when Spring gets sprung – *sprunged?, springed? sprang?*– and half the world transforms from a cold, wet and grey void into a kaleidoscopic concerto for the senses, with flowers, plants and fresh air breathing life and colour back into our lives. A period not just of rebirth and renewal, it is also a time of rememberance and to give thanks to Jesus Christ and this gorgeous world we live in and all its bountiful beauty. It's also a time to eat, and feast, and scoff, and (over) indulge in delights such as chocolate, candy, the Easter Bunny, cute little chicks, baskets and bonnets, and a whole bonanza of brilliant, bonkers and bizarre traditions, many of which date back a millennia. When it comes to enjoying ourselves, Easter really has it all.

(Let's just say what we're all thinking: Easter is better than Christmas.)

From Holy Week to Eastertide, this festive season is one of the two times a year when the secular and spiritual worlds collide in a beautiful celebration of nature and life. For over two billion Christians across the world, Easter is the most important date in their calendar and a chance to relive Christ's passion and sacrifice. For everyone else, it's a chance to embrace all that is wholesome: family, friends, feasts and hiding chocolate from the kids. Usually in our own mouths.

Welcome to *The Little Guide to Easter*. And Happy Egg Day, as the Polish say. This tiny tome is a treasure trove of wonderfully woven wit and wisdom, filled with enough Easter fun to keep you stuffed and satisfied until the Easter Bunny lays his eggs next year. Yeah, there's a few (too many) egg puns – sorry not sorry – but it's also full of historic and modern trivia, quotes and jokes to ignite your festive spirit and bring some Easter joy. It's what Jesus would have wanted.

Enjoy!

1

Here Comes the Sun

The shadows of winter are finally behind us!

With the sun putting on his shiny hat, the world awakens in a vibrant celebration of new life and hope. If only for a week.

But what a week! Easter is here… wear something nice.

A Moveable Feast

Easter's date changes annually because it's determined by the lunar calendar. Since the 4th century, Christians have celebrated Easter on the Sunday following the first full moon after the Spring Equinox, which could be any Sunday between March 22 and April 25.

This calculation, however, was historically a source of great disagreement. In the mid-7th century, two different traditions – one Roman, one Irish– used competing methods to determine the date. The dispute was finally settled at the Synod of Whitby in 664, where it was agreed to adopt the Roman method. This is the same calculation used to set the date of Easter today.

80 million

The approximate number of chocolate eggs sold in the UK every Easter.

That's 1.1* for every man, woman and child in the country.

*The 0.1 is no doubt down to nibbling a bit off somebody else's egg!

Holy Week

Easter is more than just a long weekend. It is a whole week of traditions, rituals and celebrations. We call it Holy Week.

Palm Sunday

The start of Holy Week, commemorating Jesus's triumphant entry into Jerusalem, where crowds waved palm fronds.

Holy Monday, Tuesday, and Wednesday

Days of reflection and preparation. Wednesday is sometimes called "Spy Wednesday" in remembrance of Judas Iscariot's agreement to betray Jesus.

Maundy Thursday

Commemorates the Last Supper where Jesus shared a final meal with his apostles and washed their feet.

Good Friday

A solemn day marking the crucifixion of Jesus and his death.

Holy Saturday

A day of vigil and silence, remembering Jesus in the tomb before his resurrection.

Easter Day

The most important day of the Christian year, celebrating the resurrection of Jesus Christ.

Easter Monday

Also known as "Bright Monday", this was the first of 40 days Jesus Christ spent on Earth appearing to his disciples, preaching and proving that he was alive, before ascending to Heaven.

“

It was one of those March days when the sun shines hot and the wind blows cold: when it is summer in the light, and winter in the shade.

”

Charles Dickens
Great Expectations, 1861

"

And Spring arose on
the garden fair,

Like the Spirit of Love
felt everywhere;

And each flower and herb
on Earth's dark breast

rose from the dreams
of its wintry rest.

"

Percy Bysshe Shelley

Prometheus Unbound, with Other Poems, 1820

During the Middle Ages, eggs were a forbidden food during Lent, a Christian observance lasting 40 days, from Ash Wednesday to Holy Saturday, marked by prayer, fasting, and self-denial to prepare for the celebration of Easter.

The eggs stored throughout the fast were decorated for Easter Sunday, turning them into a symbolic treat.

This tradition dates back to at least 1290, when King Edward I of England purchased 450 eggs, which were decorated with colours and gold leaf for his household.

“

Do not abandon yourselves to despair. We are an Easter people and Alleluia is our song.

”

Pope John Paul II

Homily, November 30, 1986

HOW DOES THE EASTER BUNNY STAY HEALTHY?

Hare-obics.

"There is no time like Spring,
When life's alive in everything..."

Christina Rossetti, "Spring"
1860

"All you need is love. But a little chocolate now and then doesn't hurt."

Charles M. Schulz
(attributed)

"

Who can take the sunrise, sprinkle it with dew, cover it in chocolate and a miracle or two?

"

"The Candy Man", *Willy Wonka & the Chocolate Factory*, 1971,
Lyrics by Leslie Bricusse and Anthony Newley

WHY WAS THE EGG AFRAID TO HIDE FOR THE EASTER EGG HUNT?

He was a little chicken!

WHERE'S THE BEST PLACE TO LEARN ABOUT EASTER EGGS?

The hen-cyclopedia!

10 per cent

The percentage chocolate sales for Easter Eggs make up of Britain's annual spending on chocolate!

The average Briton spends more than £325 on chocolate every year, with almost half (46 per cent) admitting they eat chocolate at least once a day. Britain's chocolate industry is worth more than £5 billion annually.

WHAT DO RABBITS SAY BEFORE THEY EAT THEIR EASTER FEAST?

"Lettuce pray."

Maundy Thursday

The fifth day of Holy Week commemorates Jesus's Last Supper, where he instituted the Eucharist – a central Christian rite that remembers Christ's final meeting with his disciples.

The term "Eucharist" comes from the Greek word *eucharistia*, meaning "thanksgiving". As recounted in Luke 22:19-20, Jesus shared bread and wine, commanding his followers to remember his sacrifice.

The day's name, Maundy, comes from the Latin for "commandment", recalling when he humbly washed his disciples' feet and gave a new commandment to love one another.

"Two thousand years ago, Jesus is crucified. Three days later, he walks out of a cave and they celebrate with chocolate bunnies and marshmallow Peeps and beautifully decorated eggs. I guess these were things Jesus loved as a child."

Billy Crystal

Still Foolin' 'Em: Where I've Been, Where I'm Going, and Where the Hell Are My Keys?, 2013

In Medieval Europe, a well-documented folk superstition claimed that any egg laid on Good Friday will turn into a diamond… but only if kept for 100 years. Let's try it!

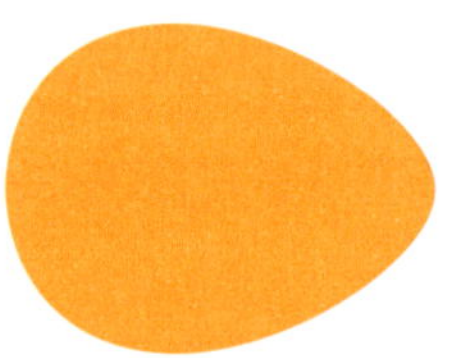

A popular 18th-century Easter entertainment in rural northern England still enjoyed today, Pace Eggs Plays were traditional folk dramas, often performed over Easter week by amateur actors.

These medieval-style mystery plays featured a theatrical fight where a hero, frequently St. George, was killed and then miraculously resurrected to defeat a villain. For their hard work, the actors were often given decorated "pace eggs" as payment – decorate, brightly dyed hard-boiled eggs.

Morris Dancing

A prominent part of Easter celebrations in the UK, Morris Dancing is a traditional English folk dance rooted in ancient pagan fertility rites that celebrate the return of spring.

Dancers, adorned with bells and ribbons, perform rhythmic routines while wielding handkerchiefs or sticks. The dance is an exuberant and symbolic welcome of new life and the triumph of spring over winter.

The Easter pot-throwing tradition in Corfu, Greece, known as the "Botides", takes place on the morning of Holy Saturday.

Residents throw large clay pots from their balconies, smashing them in the street below. The custom likely began under Venetian rule (14th century) as a New Year tradition but was adopted by Orthodox Greeks for Easter.

The loud, joyful ritual symbolizes casting out old troubles, welcoming new life, and warding off evil spirits before Christ's resurrection.

1647

The year Britain's Puritan Parliament – radical Protestants who sought to eradicate any remnants of Catholicism from the Church of England – banned all Easter (and Christmas) celebrations.

They decreed that businesses would remain open and any citizen who observed the holidays would be fined.

When Charles II's monarchy was restored in 1660 the ban was lifted.

Why was the Easter Bunny hired for the job?

He had the most eggs-perience!

In Poland, Easter Monday is known as *Śmigus-dyngus* or "Wet Monday". People playfully throw water on each other in a tradition with dual origins.

It is connected to two pagan spring rituals – symbolizing a cleansing for the new season and the baptism of Prince Mieszko I in 966, considered the official beginning of Poland as a Christian country.

Happy *Śmigus-dyngus* to you!

“There is nothing better than a friend, unless it is a friend with chocolate.”

Linda Grayson

The Friends and Lovers of Monsieur Lemaire, 1997

Good Friday

The solemn sixth day of Holy Week that commemorates Jesus Christ's crucifixion and death on the cross.

As recounted in John 19:17-30, Jesus was executed at Calvary (also known by its Aramaic name Golgotha) – a site now thought to be found within the walls of the Church of the Holy Sepulchre in the Old City of Jerusalem.

Good Friday is a day of mourning and reflection, where Christians attend special services to remember his suffering and the ultimate sacrifice he made for humanity.

Every Easter Monday, in Bessières, a town in southern France, a giant omelette is cooked using more 15,000 eggs to celebrate the end of the Lenting fast. It feeds thousands of people!

According to local legend, Napoleon and his army enjoyed an omelette in the town of Bessières. He was so impressed he ordered all the eggs from the town to be gathered to make a massive omelette for his troops.

2

Rise & Shine

After the solemnity of Good Friday and Holy Week, Easter becomes a time for joy, laughter and putting on so much weight you can no longer fit in your brand new clothes.

It's also a time to have fun, as you're about to discover...

The biggest annual social event held at the White House in Washington D.C. is the Easter Egg Roll held on Easter Monday on the South Lawn, hosted by the First Lady.

The event dates back to 1878 with President Rutherford B. Hayes. Children use a long-handled spoon to push a hard-boiled egg across the lawn in a festive race. The event is attended by the "Official White House Easter Bunny", a tradition that began in 1969 during the Nixon administration.

The identity of the Bunny is a secret.

“

Easter Sunday is the sun’s dancing day, and the earth’s holiday.

”

Nicholas Breton

“A Solemn Passion of the Soul’s Love”, 1595

In Sweden, children dress up as *Påskkärringar* ("Easter witches") on Maundy Thursday. The tradition stems from local folklore that witches flew to a legendary mountain to meet the Devil!

Dressed in old clothes, children with painted rosy cheeks carry copper kettles and birch twigs as they go door-to-door, exchanging greetings and drawings for sweets and chocolate.

“This Easter, we reflect on the brutal pain that He suffered, the scorn that He absorbed, the sins that He bore, this extraordinary gift of salvation that He gave to us. And we try, as best we can, to comprehend the darkness that He endured so that we might receive God’s light.”

Barack Obama

White House Easter Prayer Breakfast, April 7, 2015

Before the introduction of the Bank Holidays Act of 1871, Good Friday and Christmas were the *only* two days of the year recognized by English common law as national holidays – precious days off from work.

After the Act, four new bank holidays were introduced: Easter Monday, Whit Monday, the first Monday in August, and Boxing Day. Today in England, there are 10 bank holidays days in total.

The first hollow chocolate eggs were produced in 1873 by the Bristol-based chocolatiers, J.S. Fry & Sons. These early Easter eggs were made using dark chocolate, not milk, and so were a lot more bitter than today's treats.

In 1795, founder Joseph Fry – the real Willy Wonka! – patented a method of grinding cocoa beans using a steam engine. This technological breakthrough was revolutionary, enabling the mass production of chocolate for the first time.

For those hoping to conceive – eat an egg this Easter!

According to historical superstition, cooking eggs on Good Friday and consuming them on Easter Day promoted fertility.

This practice was thought to imbue the eggs with a special spiritual power!

Every year, a now-legendary Easter egg-rolling competition is held on Vale Street in Bristol, UK, the birthplace of the chocolate Easter egg.

For over 20 years, hundreds of participants have rolled eggs down England's steepest street, with its challenging 22-degree gradient. The tradition of egg rolling at Easter dates back to the 17th century, and symbolizes the stone being rolled away from Jesus's tomb.

The winner is theowner of the egg that travels the furthest... without cracking, of course.

In Bermuda, handmade kites fill the sky on Good Friday. The tradition is believed to have started when a teacher used a kite to explain Christ's ascension to heaven to his students.

Today, these colorful, hexagonal kites, symbolize Jesus rising from the dead and are flown in parks and on beaches in a joyful celebration.

April 23

1564 and 1616

The world's greatest wordsmith, William Shakespeare, is believed to have been born and to have died on the same date.

This fateful day has most often fallen on Easter Day too, turning the celebration of his life and death into an even more remarkable – and fittingly theatrical – event of resurrection and rebirth.

A poetic coincidence that would no doubt have tickled Shakespeare himself.

86 per cent

The percentage of UK adults who celebrated Easter in 2025 – 46 million people!

WHY SHOULDN'T YOU TELL AN EASTER EGG A JOKE?

It might crack up!

Easter Sunday

The final day of Holy Week marks the joyous celebration of Jesus' resurrection from the dead. After his crucifixion on the Cross, his body was laid in a tomb sealed by a stone and guarded by Roman soldiers.

On Sunday morning, as recounted in Matthew 28:1-10, women who went to the tomb found the stone rolled away and were told by an angel, "He is not here; he has risen!" Jesus later appeared to his followers, confirming God had resurrected him, a miracle celebrated as the foundation of Christian faith.

March 31

1918

Easter Day – and the day that Daylight Saving Time (DST) was first implemented in the US, as part of the Standard Time Act of 1918. The measure was a temporary initiative designed to conserve fuel and energy during World War I.

Though the act was repealed after the conflict, the concept was resurrected for World War II and today remains become a permanent feature of American, and British, life.

If you've ever wondered why films have "Easter eggs" – small hidden details in a shot waiting to be noticed by eagle-eyed fans – the term came from *The Rocky Horror Picture Show.*

During filming, crew members would hide Easter* eggs around the set as part of an Easter egg hunt, to provide entertainment for the cast between shot set-ups. Some eggs can be seen in the film – if you look closely enough.

*In true zany *Rocky Horror* form, the film was actually shot from October to December, spanning both Halloween and Christmas – not Easter!

Popular since the Middle Ages, the ancient tradition of "Heaving" on Easter Monday and Tuesday remains a common sight today in Northern England.

To participate in heaving, husbands lift their wives in a chair – similar to giving someone "birthday bumps" – on Easter Monday. Women then reciprocate the act on Tuesday.

Rooted in pagan rituals and since reinterpreted by Christians, heaving symbolizes the rising of Christ from the tomb.

Check the date!

To keep you from getting confused every year, here's every Easter Sunday date for the next decade. You're welcome.

2026: April 5	**2031: April 13**
2027: March 28	**2032: March 28**
2028: April 16	**2033: April 17**
2029: April 1	**2034: April 9**
2030: April 21	**2035: March 25**

Bottle Kicking

Britain's weirdest sport – think Rugby with food instead of a ball – the bizarre "bottle kicking" is a tradition that began in the late 18th century when a startled hare distracted a bull from charging two ladies out walking in Hallaton, Leicestershire, UK on Easter Monday.

To give thanks, the ladies donated money to the church to provide the poor of Hallaton with a hare pie and ale, 12 loaves of bread and two barrels of beer each Easter Monday. When villagers from neughbouring Medbourne tried to steal this feast, a fight broke out. This rivalry has now evolved into an annual contest between the two villages who compete over pieces of cooked hare pie before trying to kick three barrels of beer, known as bottles, from a starting field to their own village – by any means possible!

Winners get to keep the beer.

In Greece, the festive game of Tsougrisma is played on Easter Sunday after midnight mass.

The hard-boiled eggs symbolize the sealed tomb of Christ, and the cracking of an egg represents his resurrection.

Players tap their red-dyed eggs together, and whoever's egg remains uncracked is declared the winner, believed to have good luck for the entire year.

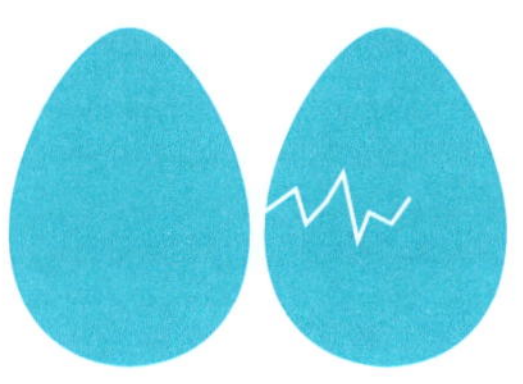

The legend of the Easter Bunny originated in Germany, where it was known as the "Osterhase" or Easter Hare.

First mentioned in late 16th-century German writings, the hare was a pagan symbol of fertility and new life due to its prolific breeding, linking it to the spring season.

This tradition was brought to America in the 18th century by German immigrants to Pennsylvania, where the rabbit's role evolved into a benevolent judge who delivered coloured eggs to well-behaved children on Easter Sunday.

The world's most popular chocolate for Easter Egg hunts are Cadbury Creme Eggs – they make up 63.5 per cent of all egg sales!

More than 1.5 million are produced every day. If all the Cadbury Creme Eggs produced in a year were piled on top of each other, they would be *3,500 times* higher than Mount Everest!

In 2025, the average spend by Britons on Easter gifts for family or friends was £37. That's approximately enough to buy 43 Cadbury Creme Eggs – just don't eat them all at once!

“

Jesus said to her [Martha],
‘I am the resurrection and the life.
The one who believes in me
will live, even though they die;
and whoever lives by believing in
me will never die. Do you
believe this?’

”

John 11:25-26

The legendary Fabergé eggs – 50 jewelled, decorative eggs created by the House of Fabergé and renowned for their intricate craftsmanship and opulence – began as a magnificent Easter gift.

In 1885, Russian Tsar Alexander III commissioned a gold and enamel egg for his wife, which opened to reveal a golden chicken. This breathtaking egg within an egg became a cherished tradition, with each annual creation symbolizing the preciousness and joy of Easter.

In 2007, the most expensive Fabergé egg – the Rothschild – sold at Christie's for £8.9 million!

Pysanka

The Ukrainian word for a decorated egg. The term comes from the Ukrainian verb *pysaty*, which means "to write".

Since pagan times, Ukrainians have made pysanka as a way to symbolise health and fertility. This tradition was later adopted by Christians to symbolize the resurrection of Christ.

It flourished in the US following Ukrainian immigration, becoming a widely cherished cultural custom.

Spring Songs:
A PLAYLIST

"Spring Is Here" – Nina Simone

"Here Comes The Sun" – The Beatles

"Dry The Rain" – Beta Band

"When Its Springtime in Alaska" – Johnny Cash

"Mr Blue Sky" – Electric Light Orchestra

"Waiting For The Sun" – The Doors

"Sunny Afternoon" – The Kinks

"Flowers" – Miley Cyrus

"In Bloom" – Nirvana

In Australia, the Easter Bilby is the popular alternative to the Easter Bunny, born from a conservation initiative in the 1970s.

The long-eared, native marsupial replaces the rabbit, which is an invasive pest that threatens the native bilby's natural habitat.

In 1859, Thomas Austin brought 24 rabbits to Australia from England for hunting purposes. They quickly multiplied and spread across the continent. Within three years, Austin's rabbits had multiplied into the thousands.

Today, it is one of the most destructive biological invasions in history!

“

The egg
is the symbol of
perfection.

”

Mason Cooley

City Aphorisms, Vol. 1, 1989.

3

Hot Cross Bunnies

Hot Cross Buns are the perfect metaphor for Easter.

They're a delicious sweet treat (especially with butter and jam and a cup of tea). They also remind us what Easter is about: Jesus Christ's passion, death and resurrection.

For balance, this chapter's full of wit and wisdom about both...

The word "Easter" likely originated from *Eostre*, the Anglo-Saxon goddess of dawn and spring.

This theory was first recorded by the Venerable Bede, an 8th-century English monk. He wrote that the spring festival of Eostre was so ingrained in the culture that her name became the one used for the Christian celebration of the Resurrection.

In a tradition unique to France, it is not an animal such as a Bunny that delivers eggs, it is the Easter Bells – flying church bells known as "les cloches de Pâques".

According to legend, these bells fly to Rome to be blessed by the Pope after Good Friday. They then return with wings on Easter Sunday, ringing loudly as they fly over the country while dropping chocolate eggs and other treats for children!

WHAT DO YOU GET IF YOU POUR HOT WATER DOWN A RABBIT HOLE?

Hot cross bunnies!

Similar to leaving mince pies and milk for Santa and Rudolf, children sometimes leave carrots out for the Easter Bunny.

The tradition is based on the idea that the carrots are a snack to energize the bunny as he hops around delivering eggs and treats to everyone ahead of Easter Day. Have you left your carrots out?

10 per cent

The percentage of Britons who celebrate Easter as an entirely religious holiday, according to a 2020 YouGov Study.

1897

The year that Chocolate Easter eggs were first made with milk chocolate, and the famous Cadbury's Dairy Milk Chocolate was first introduced.

Today, 80 per cent of all Easter eggs are made using milk chocolate.

38 per cent

The percentage of an Easter egg that is chocolate.

The rest is cardboard packaging.

The earliest decorated eggs were found at at the Diepkloof Rock Shelter in South Africa. They were believed to be 60,000-year-old engraved ostrich eggshells!

Used as ancient water containers by Middle Stone Age humans, the shells bear abstract, geometric patterns, thought to be one of the earliest forms of visual art that humans ever produced.

5,000lbs

The weight of the world's largest Easter egg – the Vegreville Pysanka, a sculpture in Alberta, Canada. This is the same weight as an SUV!

Standing 31 feet tall, this monument is an engineering marvel. It is made from 3,500 interlocking pieces of aluminum, took 12,000 hours to build, and was dedicated to the town's Ukrainian community.

78 per cent

The percentage of Americans who eat the ears first on their chocolate Easter bunnies, according to the National Confectioners Association, 2023. Just 5 per cent eat the tail first.

In the United States, 90 million chocolate bunnies are sold each year.

Lilium longiflorum

The Latin name of the most popular Easter flower, the white Easter Lily, a species native to the Ryukyu Islands of southern Japan and Taiwan.

A common Easter decoration symbolizing the purity of Christ and representing rebirth and hope, its pristine white, trumpet-shaped bloom is said to represent the trumpet of the angel Gabriel announcing Jesus's rebirth, while legend says the lilies grew in the Garden of Gethsemane where Christ's tears of sorrow fell. The flowers are used to adorn churches and homes as a beautiful sign of the new life promised by Easter.

Believe it or not, another common Easter food is...

PRETZELS!

Their connection to Easter dates back to 7th-century Europe when monks twisted leftover dough into a shape resembling a child's arms folded in prayer, which they then baked. The soft, warm treats were given to children as a reward for learning their prayers.

This tradition is why many German families still eat pretzels and hard-boiled eggs as their main Easter meal on Good Friday.

Crime fiction is a central part of Easter in Norway, a tradition known as *Påskekrim* (Easter Crime).

The phenomenon was sparked by the February 1923 publication of *Bergenstoget plyndret i natt* (The Bergen Line Robbery), written by Nordahl Grieg and Nils Lie. The publisher famously ran a large advertisement on the front page of a major newspaper with the headline "Bergen train looted in the night" leading many readers to believe a real train robbery had occurred.

The clever marketing stunt was a huge success, and the tradition of reading crime novels at Easter was born.

Easter is also an opportunity for a cabin holiday (*hytte*) in Norway, where families head to the mountains or sea.

This tradition is why *Påske* is so popular! A typical Easter weekend involves a blend of skiing in the winter sun, reading a new detective novel, and eating oranges or *Kvikk Lunsj*.

Endless
Amounts of
Sugar
To
Eat and
Regret

The tradition of baking special buns on Good Friday is centuries old.

The cross on the bun symbolizes the crucifixion of Christ, and there were early beliefs that these buns possessed miraculous powers. It was thought they would never go mouldy could cure diseases, and would protect homes from misfortune.

In the early 18th century, they became known as Hot Cross Buns and were sold by London street vendors.

In Christian tradition, Jesus is referred to as the "Lamb of God". This title, used by John the Baptist in the Gospel of John (1:29), links Jesus' sacrifice to the Old Testament practice of animal sacrifice for the atonement of sins. It's why lamb, for centuries, lamb was the chosen meat to roast on Easter Day.

Today, just under a third of British families eat lamb for their Easter meal.

2.4 billion

The number of
Christians
who celebrate Easter
worldwide.

8.8

The average number of Easter eggs a child in Britain receives every Easter.

At 1,000 calories per egg, this is double their recommended calorie intake for a whole week solely on chocolate!

“

It was a lover and his lass,
With a hey, and a ho, and a hey nonino,
That o'er the green corn-field did pass,
In the spring time, the only pretty ring time,
When birds do sing, hey ding a ding, ding;
Sweet lovers love the spring.

”

William Shakespeare

As You Like It, in Act V, Scene 3, 1599

On Easter Sunday, thousands of pilgrims gather in St. Peter's Square in the Vatican City, Italy, to hear the Pope deliver his special "Urbi et Orbi" blessing.

Delivered from the central balcony of St. Peter's Basilica, the address, meaning "to the city and to the world" is a solemn message of hope and peace that is broadcast around the world.

“

Love has triumphed over hatred, light over darkness and truth over falsehood. Forgiveness has triumphed over revenge. Evil has not disappeared from history; it will remain until the end, but it no longer has the upper hand; it no longer has power over those who accept the grace of this Easter day.

”

“Urbi et Orbi”, Easter message of his Holiness Pope Francis, Saint Peter’s Square, Sunday, 20 April 2025

70 per cent

The percentage of Easter treats consumed in America in 2025 that was chocolate.

In the U.S. Easter chocolate sales is a $2.1 billion industry annually with Americans consuming more than 73 million lbs of chocolate at Easter – the second biggest chocolate-selling holiday in the US after Halloween.

The famous Pacific island of Rapa Nui was named Easter Island by Dutch explorer Jacob Roggeveen, who first sighted it on Easter Sunday in 1722.

While Roggeveen named the island, it had been inhabited for more than a millennia by its indigenous people, who were responsible for creating the island's now world-famous moai statues.

"

And on that day, when they have a new fire in every parish, all the old fires shall be put out, and the houses shall be clean. And then they shall light the new fire, and bring it to their houses, and light their candles with it, and make merry.

"

John Mirk

Festial, c.1380s. (He's talking about Easter)

“

My favorite Catholic holiday is Easter. For those of you that don’t know, Easter is the day we celebrate Jesus rising from the grave and coming back to Earth as a rabbit that hides coloured eggs.

”

Adam Ferrara

Comedy Central Presents Adam Ferrera, 2003

"

Easter is...

Joining in a birdsong,

Eying an early sunrise,

Smelling yellow daffodils,

Unbolting windows and doors,

Skipping through meadows,

Cuddling newborns,

Hoping, believing,

Reviving spent life,

Inhaling fresh air,

Sprinkling seeds along furrows,

Tracking in the mud.

Easter is the soul's first taste of spring.

"

Richelle E. Goodrich

Making Wishes, 2015

Hot cross buns!
Hot cross buns!
One a penny, two a penny,
Hot cross buns!

If you have no daughters,
Give them to your sons.
One a penny, two a penny,
Hot cross buns!

The term "hot cross bun" first appeared in print in 1733 in *Poor Robin's Almanac*, which featured the famous rhyme above about an old woman selling them.

4

Spring Has Sprung

The days grow longer, the air warms, and the world transforms.

From blooming flowers and chirping birds to ancient (and bonkers) traditions, Easter is really just a dressed-up celebration of Spring.

This chapter is a fresh start and should put a spring in your step...

Wesołego jajka!

A common Easter greeting in Poland that means "Happy egg!". It is often used as an alternative to the mealy mouthful – "*Wesołych Świąt Wielkanocnych*" (Happy Easter).

Wesołego jajka is pronounced, carefully: veh-soh-weh-goh-yuy-kah.

Hocktide, a medieval English festival, was once celebrated on the Monday and Tuesday after the second Sunday following Easter.

It was the first major festival day after Lent and was a time for sports and games, as well as a day for the collection and payment of rents and dues.

Today, the tradition is only observed as Tutti Day in the town of Hungerford, Berkshire, when "Tutti-men", dressed in top hats and tails, go around handing out oranges.*

*We swear: we're not making this up.

Since 1779, the Easter weekend in Workington, Cumbria, has been marked by a mass rough-and-tumble rugby-based game called "Uppies and Downies".

The teams, based on which side of town you're from, have no rules and vie to get a specially-made leather ball in to their respective goals: Workington Hall for the Uppies or the harbour for the Downies.

Whose side are you on?

“

No winter lasts forever; no spring skips its turn.

”

Hal Borland

Sundial of the Seasons, 1972

"Spring is the time of plans and projects."

Konstantin Levin

Anna Karenina, Leo Tolstoy, 1878

“

He is not here; he has risen! Remember how he told you, while he was still with you in Galilee: ‘The Son of Man must be delivered over to the hands of sinners, be crucified and on the third day be raised again.’

”

Luke 24: 6–7

Painted by Leonardo da Vinci from 1495-1498, *The Last Supper* depicts Jesus' final meal with his apostles on Maundy Thursday. This masterpiece captures the dramatic moment he reveals one will betray him (spoiler: Judas), the event that leads to Christ's crucifixion on Good Friday.

Da Vinci used a technique called "one-point perspective" to create an astonishing illusion of depth. To do this, he hammered a nail into the wall at the exact focal point – Jesus' temple –and then used strings to precisely guide the lines of the room, ensuring that every element of the painting draws the viewer's eye directly to Christ.

The name Good Friday has two key meanings. Linguistically, "good" is thought to derive from an archaic sense meaning "holy", a usage still seen in phrases such as "the good book". Therefore, "Good Friday" would have originally meant "Holy Friday".

Theologically, the day is also considered "good" because it commemorates Jesus' crucifixion, which Christians believe was a necessary sacrifice – a good thing – for the atonement of human sin and the ultimate triumph over death.

Triduum

The Latin term to mean "three days".

The Easter Triduum commemorates the three central events of the Christian faith: Jesus' Passion (the final period of his life) death and resurrection – referring to Good Friday, Holy Saturday and Easter Sunday.

Held after sunset on Holy Saturday and before dawn on Easter Sunday, the Easter Vigil is the first official celebration of Jesus' Resurrection. It marks the transition from the solemn Good Friday to the joyful Easter Sunday.

The Vigil is divided into four parts and the jubilant "Alleluia" is sung for the first time since the beginning of Lent.

"In the spring, at the end of the day, you should smell like dirt."

Margaret Atwood
Bluebeard's Egg, 1983

"From you have I been absent in the spring,
When proud-pied April, dressed in all his trim,
Hath put a spirit of youth in everything."

William Shakespeare

"Sonnet 98", 1609

16.72 meters (54 ft 10 in)

The current Guinness World Record for the largest decorated Easter egg! The eggs-traordinary record was broken in Pomerode, Brazil, in 2023.

To put it in perspective, it's bigger than three giraffes standing on top of each other!

WHY DO YOU NEED AN EASTER EGG HUNTING LICENSE?

Because no poaching is allowed!

"

Spring is the sun shining on the rain and the rain falling on the the sunshine.

"

Mary

The Secret Garden, Frances Hodgson Burnett, 1911

In 12 of Germany's 16 states, public dancing at nightclubs is prohibited on Good Friday.

This ban, known as "Tanzverbot", respects the religious solemnity of the day, mourning the crucifixion of Jesus. Even Europe's clubbing capital, Berlin, becomes a dance-free zone out of respect for the religious day.

Until 9pm, at least. Violators can face fines of up to €1,500.

Several flowers are traditionally associated with Easter.

If you plan to arrange a pretty bouquet for your Easter basket this year try the traditional combination of Easter lily, hyacinths, carnations, lilacs, daffodils, tulips, stocks, baby's breath and green foliage.

“

How lovely yellow is! It stands for the sun.

”

Vincent Van Gogh

Easter Eggs
are proof that God
loves us and wants us
to be happy.

On Easter Monday, April 21, 2025, Pope Francis died at age 88 at his Vatican residence.

While his passing on Easter Monday is deeply symbolic for Christians, he is not the only pope to have died at Easter.

Pope John Paul II passed away on April 2, 2005, which was the Vigil of the Easter Octave (Divine Mercy Sunday).

Being born on Easter Day is a rare event that cannot be predicted, as the holiday's date changes annually.

For many, it's a special occasion that ties their birthday to themes of new life and renewal. It's also an interesting conversation starter, with many "Easter babies" joking about being the reincarnation of Jesus!

The most famous people born on Easter Day are:

Eric Idle (1943)
Dianne Wiest (1948)
Quentin Tarantino (1963)
Mariah Carey (1970)
Emma Watson (1990)

"The Easter bunny ate all of the carrots we left him. What a pig!"

Steve Carrell

"

Spring drew on: she was indeed already come; the frosts of winter had ceased; its snows were melted, its cutting winds ameliorated.

"

Jane Eyre

Jane Eyre, Charlotte Bronte, 1847

"Blossom by blossom the spring begins."

Algernon Charles Swinburne

Atalanta in Calydon, 1865

"

In your Easter bonnet,
with all the frills upon it,
you'll be the grandest lady
in the Easter parade.

"

Bing Crosby

"Easter Parade", *As Thousands Cheer*, 1933.
Written by Irving Berlin

The Easter bonnet tradition dates back to medieval Europe, where new clothes symbolized spiritual renewal. Bonnets appeared in the 13th century, becoming elaborate and floral-adorned during the Victorian era. The tradition was cemented by the New York City Easter Parade and Irving Berlin's song, "Easter Parade", making the hat an iconic symbol of spring and new life.

“If winter comes, can spring be far behind?”

Percy Bysshe Shelley

"Ode to the West Wind", 1819

“

In Alsace and neighboring regions, these eggs are called rabbit eggs because of the myth told to fool simple people and children that the Easter Bunny is going around laying eggs and hiding them in the herb gardens. So the children look for them, even more enthusiastically, to the delight of smiling adults.

”

Georg Franck von Franckenau

De ovis paschalibus ("About Easter eggs"), 1682

* Von Franckenau's essay contains the first written reference to both an Easter egg hunt and the Easter hare.

The modern idea of the Easter egg hunt has its roots in Germany.

Men would hide the eggs for the women and children to find, a nod to the story of the resurrection, in which Jesus' empty tomb was discovered by women.

The tradition was brought to the United States by German immigrants in the 18th century.

5

Heavenly Chocolate

Step into a world of pure indulgence and delight – its time to gorge on the real meaning of Easter: chocolate. Just kidding.

This chapter celebrates the passion, rise and glory of Easter chocolate, from the first eggs, the ascension of the Easter Bunny (who lays eggs?), and why these sweet treats have become an essential part of our holiday celebration. Open wide...

“

Happy Easter everyone! Jesus dies, comes back from the dead – and we get chocolate eggs. It’s like turn-down service from God.

”

Denis Leary
No Cure for Cancer, 2004

81 per cent

The percentage of parents who admit to stealing* chocolate from their children's Easter eggs, according to a 2024 survey by the National Confectioners Association of America.

*The other 19 percent of parents probably don't think it counts as stealing as they bought it in the first place.

$100 billion

The value of the global chocolate confectionary market – an 100 per cent increase from $52 billion in 2002.

336 million

The total number of hot cross buns consumed in the UK over the Easter season in 2024, according to a report by ALDI UK Press Office.

That means the average Brit eats at least five hot cross buns a year – with 1 in 7 consuming more than 10.

Eastertide

The Easter season, or Eastertide, is a 50-day period of profound joy in the Christian liturgical calendar.

Beginning on Easter Sunday, it celebrates Jesus' Resurrection, his ascension into heaven and the gift of new life.

The season culminates on Pentecost Sunday, a name derived from the Greek word for "fiftieth", which commemorates the descent of the Holy Spirit – the active presence of God in the world and in the lives of believers.

“During our breakfast and after, the Children hunted for Easter eggs, it being Maundy Thursday, and they were in the greatest delight.”

Queen Victoria

Diary entry, 1848

"Didst thou not fall out with a tailor for wearing his new doublet before Easter?"

Mercutio to Benvolio

Romeo and Juliet, Act 3, Scene I,
William Shakespeare, 1594

1 in 70

The odds of Easter falling on 19 April, the date that Easter falls on most frequently in the Gregorian calendar. This is a consequence of Easter falling on the first Sunday after the first full moon that occurs on or after the spring equinox (March 21).

Due to the complex interplay of lunar cycles and calendar dates, April 19 simply happens to be the date that most often falls within that specific set of conditions.

* April 19 is the day the The Battles of Lexington and Concord took place, FYI, long considered the start of the American Revolutionary War.

“

Here comes Peter Cottontail, hopping down the bunny trail, hippity-hoppity, Easter's on its way, bringing every girl and boy, baskets full of Easter joy, things to make your Easter bright and gay.

”

Steve Nelson and Jack Rollins

"Here Comes Peter Cottontail", 1950

“

I’ve read the Bible.
I can’t find
the word ‘bunny’
or ‘chocolate’
anywhere.

”

Bill Hicks

Relentless, 1992

April 7, AD 30

The date of the very first Easter Day.

Based on scholars studies and astronomical calculations, it is believed to be the date that Jesus was crucified.

On the Holy Saturday night before Easter, known as *Osternacht*, communities across northern Germany light huge bonfires.

This ancient tradition, with both pagan and Christian roots, symbolizes the end of winter and the arrival of spring.

The fires are also believed to ward off evil spirits and celebrate the light of the resurrected Jesus.

“

Good idea: finding the Easter eggs on Easter.

Bad idea: finding the Easter eggs on Christmas.

”

Jack Handey

Deep Thoughts, 1992

Similar to the blooming of billions of flowers, the Easter season is famed for its use of pastel colours, with each one taking on its own purpose and significance:

White: light, triumph and glory.

Violet: penance, power, and royalty.

Pink: joy and love.

Green: hope and eternal life.

Red: sacrifice, blood and martyrdom.

Gold: majesty, glory and divinity.

Blue: Hope, expectation and new beginnings.

"

How do you get Crucifixion, Resurrection and then chocolate bunnies and coloured eggs? How do you do that one? Even kids are going, 'Rabbits don't lay eggs. What is this?'

"

Robin Williams

Live on Broadway, 2002

“

Easter is meant to be a symbol of hope, renewal, and new life.

”

Janine di Giovanni

Easter, Not Christmas, Is the True Celebration of Hope, *Newsweek*, April 2017

Sort of Good

In the US, Good Friday is a federal holiday, but only in a handful states. In these states, government offices and courts are closed for the day.

Currently, 12 US states officially observe Good Friday as a holiday: Connecticut, Delaware, Florida, Hawaii, Indiana, Kentucky (half-day holiday), Louisiana, New Jersey, North Carolina, North Dakota, Tennessee and Texas.

WHAT DO YOU CALL THE EASTER BUNNY WITH FLEAS?

Bugs Bunny!

In 2016, a burglar broke into Brighton chocolatiers Choccywoccydodah. The thief stole £60 from the till but completely overlooked the most valuable items on display: a trio of Fabergé-inspired Easter eggs.

Valued at an astonishing £25,000 for the set, each egg weighed 100 kg, and were 3-foot tall! The incident became a worldwide headline story. "The thief obviously is not a chocolate lover," the owners of Choccywoccydodah said after the break-in.

"Easter is a time for dressing up, looking your best, and hunting for candy. It's Halloween in reverse."

Melanie White

A Mom's Guide to..., 2007

Easter egg hunts were far more widespread in the early 1900s. In 1902 Hamley's advertised an "Easter Egg Hunt Box" in *The Gentlewoman*, calling it "A Novelty for Children's Parties given at Easter-tide."

The box contained eggs and a hare, which were "all hidden in suitable places and the children are sent to hunt for them, 3 of the Eggs contain Coupons, first, second, and third prizes, the others are filled with little Trinkets and Toys."

In parts of Germany, the Easter Bunny is not the only animal that delivers eggs. In some regions, especially in the state of Westphalia, the eggs might be delivered by the Easter Fox (*Osterfuchs*) or the Easter Rooster (*Osterhahn*).

The tradition of the fox is thought to have a connection to the custom of using onion skins to dye eggs a reddish-brown color, which resembled the color of a fox.

For centuries in parts of England, particularly Cambridge and Brighton, people would gather on Good Friday to take part in a unique community tradition: communal skipping.

Men, women and children would mark the start of the Easter weekend by jumping over long lengths of rope, often fishing lines. The event was sometimes known as "long rope day".

While it was a form of celebration – the skipping over of sins – some later speculated that the long rope was associated with the legend that Judas hanged himself with rope after betraying Christ.

"Easter is seen as a time of spiritual preparation for the day we later celebrate and welcome the 'grand miracle' Christ accomplish through the cross."

C.S. Lewis

The Grand Miracle, 1945

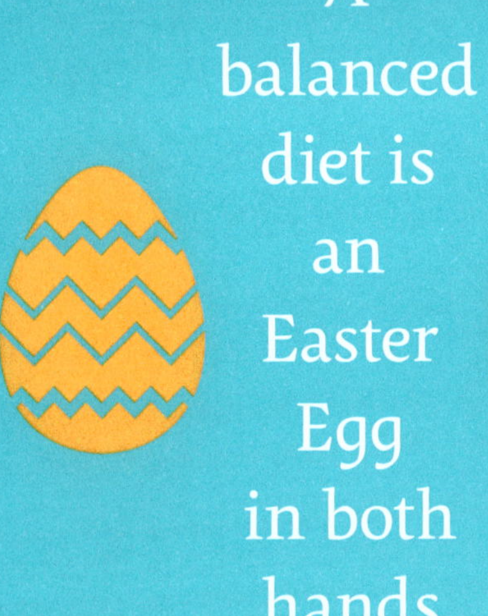

A
balanced
diet is
an
Easter
Egg
in both
hands.

Spring Songs:
EASTER PLAYLIST

"Chocolate Jesus" – Tom Waits

"Egg Race" – The Specials

"Basket of Eggs" – The Low Anthem

"White Rabbit" – Jefferson Airplane

"Mary Had a Little Lamb" – Stevie Ray Vaughan

"Easter Sunday" – Jethro Tull

"Resurrection" – Michael Jackson

"Hallelujah" – Jeff Buckley

"The Cross" – Prince

Easter: your favorite excuse to eat chocolate for every meal.

New Clothes

The tradition of wearing new clothes on Easter dates back centuries, and can be traced to spring's pagan renewal and the Resurrection's spiritual rebirth.

This custom evolved into the famous New York Easter Parade.

In the late 19th century, people would celebrate Christ's resurrection by spontaneously walking down Fifth Avenue after church, showcasing (read: strutting) their expensive and elaborate new outfits and bonnets in a grand social procession.

6

Back to the Egg

Hunts, rolls, jarps, races, decorations and dyes – Easter Eggs come in all shapes and sizes. Before the bunnies, baskets and bonnets, there was the egg, a powerful symbol of new life and the empty tomb.

Let's celebrate the glory of these crackin' little icons. How do you eat yours?

Easter Egg hunts are proof that your children can find things without having to be asked 1,000 times first.

25

The number of Cadbury's Mini-Eggs in a standard 80g bag, America's No.1 chocolate Easter Egg treat.

501,000

The number of eggs found in the the world's largest hunt. The hunt took place at at the Cypress Gardens Adventure Park in Winter Haven, Florida, on 1 April 2007.

9,753 children took part. Naturally, it took them just 60 minutes to find them all.

In some regions of Switzerland, the Easter Cuckoo is a figure in local folklore.

Instead of the Easter Bunny, the cuckoo is believed to be the one who delivers and hides Easter eggs.

The cuckoo, of course, is one of the first birds to return in spring, so is seen as a symbol of new beginnings.

"Thousands of eggs were rolled in every direction, children were everywhere laughing and capering in infantile pleasure, the elders were looking on with a more staid and demure, but not less hearty enjoyment, and altogether the scene was one of the strangest and yet most thoroughly happy and enjoyable that I have seen for years."

Egg Rolling Event,
Preston, *Lancashire Post*, 1867

"

If I'd have known becoming a priest would entail dressing up in Easter Bunny costume, I'd have had a complete rethink and taken up prostitution. As indeed my headmistress originally suggested! Mind you, I'd probably have ended up in a rabbit costume then as well.

"

Geraldine Granger

"The Easter Bunny", *Vicar of Dibley*, 1996

Nesting

At Easter, the tradition of weaving baskets dates back to the Middle Ages and were designed to represent birds' nests, a powerful symbol of new life and fertility.

Traditionally woven from materials like wicker, they complete their meaning when filled with eggs, symbolizing rebirth and the promise of spring that comes with the Easter season.

Simnel cake is a medieval fruit cake, dating back at least as far as 1475.

It is topped with eleven marzipan balls to symbolize Jesus' apostles, with Judas excluded for his betrayal.

Originally a treat for Mothering Sunday, the cake has since become a cherished part of modern Easter traditions.

WHAT DO YOU CALL THE EASTER BUNNY THE DAY AFTER EASTER?

Eggshausted.

Hot cross buns are a significant Easter treat. But did you know that the spices contained within – like cinnamon and nutmeg – were originally used to symbolize the dark embalming spices used on Jesus' body after his crucifixion.

49

The number of Easter Eggs smashed alternately in 30 seconds by a team of two – a Guinness World Record!

The feat was achieved by Sam Thompson and Pete Wicks for the *Staying Relevant* podcast, in London, UK, on 16 April 2025.

"Christ the Lord is risen today,
sons of men and angels say.

Raise your joys and triumphs
high; sing, ye heavens and
earth reply."

Charles Wesley

"Christ the Lord Is Risen Today", 1739

The world's largest hot cross bun was a colossal creation, weighing 168 kg (370 lb 6 oz) and measuring a massive 8ft in diameter!

It was baked in Bolton on April 5, 2012, by Greenhalghs Bakery. It took two hours to cook – a normal bun takes 10 minutes.

The bun was so huge that it could make over 1,500 regular-sized hot cross buns!

1,170,000kWh

The amount of energy it requires to recycle every piece of Easter egg packaging in the UK, roughly 8,000 tonnes of packaging waste.

That's enough energy to hard boil more than 180,000 eggs!

"

'Twas Easter-Sunday. The full-blossomed trees filled all the air with fragrance and with joy.

"

Henry Wadsworth Longfellow

"The Song of Hiawatha", 1855

1.182 trillion

The current level of global annual egg production, an industry worth more than $310 billion in 2025.

These eggs come from approx. 6.4 billion laying hens.

If you were to lay all these eggs end-to-end they would circle the Earth's equator an incredible 3,500 times!

For Christians, the chick emerging from an egg is a powerful metaphor for the resurrection of Jesus Christ.

The egg represents the sealed tomb, and the chick breaking free symbolizes Jesus rising from the grave, triumphing over death and offering new life to believers. This symbolism is deepened by the chick's colour –yellow – the quintessential colour of spring.

As one of the first colours to appear in nature with the arrival of daffodils and crocuses, yellow is a natural sign of new beginnings and rebirth, mirroring the central message of Easter.

“

Easter is the only time when it’s perfectly safe to put all your eggs in one basket.

”

Evan Esar

Esar’s Comic Dictionary, 1943

Chocolate Martini

Dive into the Easter spirit even more with this divine cocktail...

Ingredients

200ml gin
50g dark chocolate
100ml chocolate liqueur
crushed ice

Make it Right

Measure out 200ml gin in a jug. Melt 50g dark chocolate and pour into the gin. Whisk until smooth. Add 100ml chocolate liqueur. For each cocktail, shake 100ml of the chocolate liquid with crushed ice and strain into a martini glass. Decorate with a curl of lemon zest.

“The wise man puts all his eggs in one basket and watches the basket.”

Andrew Carnegie

1592

The year Queen Elizabeth I banned, by law, the sale of Hot Cross Buns! The law was a decree from the London Clerk of Markets as part of the Protestant Reformation. Spiced, cross-marked buns were seen as too closely associated with Catholicism and were therefore considered a form of religious superstition. The Monarch's decree strictly limited the sale of these buns to just Good Friday, Christmas and funerals. Baking them at home, however, was not outlawed, which allowed the tradition to continue and eventually thrive once again.

In Greece, Easter is celebrated with exclusively red eggs, a tradition rich in symbolism.

The color represents the blood of Christ and the triumph of life over death, while the egg itself is an ancient emblem of renewal.

This powerful custom serves to celebrate the core message of the Resurrection.

While no animal delivers eggs in Italy, the dove (*Colomba*) is a significant Easter symbol.

The traditional Italian Easter cake, called Colomba di Pasqua, is baked in the shape of a dove to represent peace and new beginnings.

This sweet, yeasted bread is typically enjoyed on Easter Sunday, symbolizing hope and the Holy Spirit.

86 per cent

The percentage of adults in the United States who spring cleaned their house in 2025, according to the American Cleaning Institute.

The history of spring cleaning dates back to the Persian spring festival of Nowruz, which marks the first day of spring, and involves a practice called *khaneh takani* (shaking the house).

The term "spring cleaning" was first officially recorded in the 1800s.

Jarping

Have you ever jarped?

No! You must. Egg Jarping is a traditional Easter game played in NorthEast England where two players use decorated, hard-boiled eggs. Think conkers. But with eggs. They tap the eggs together, with the aim of cracking their opponent's shell while keeping their own intact. Whoever's cracks first, loses.

On Easter Monday 2019, the UK experienced its hottest Easter on record. Temperatures in all four nations of the UK surpassed previous records with the highest temperature peaking at 25°C (77°F).

This exceptionally warm weather was attributed to high pressure and winds drawing in warm air from the continent. In April, the average daytime temperature in England is around 14°C (57°F).

Palm Sunday

The first day of Holy Week commemorates Jesus' entry into Jerusalem on a donkey. As recounted in Matthew 21:1–11, crowds shouted "Hosanna!" and laid palm branches on his path.

Today, palm crosses are given on Palm Sunday to remind Christians of his triumphant entry into the Holy Land and his impending sacrifice.

Easter Clipping

An ancient English folk custom, Easter Clipping involves participants holding hands and forming a human chain around their church in a symbolic "clipping" or embrace.

On Easter Day, this communal act represented the unity of the congregation and their love for their church on the church's most important day.

In the 16th century, before England's break with Rome, Pope Clement VII sent Henry VIII a symbolic Easter gift. A hard-boiled egg, symbolizing rebirth, was presented to the king in an ornate silver container.

This diplomatic gesture was made during a period of growing tension between the English monarchy and the Papacy, just before Henry's quest for an annulment from first wife, Catherine of Aragon, led to the English Reformation.

"The very first Easter taught us this: that life never ends and love never dies."

Kate McGahan

Only Gone from Your Sight, 2014

Please, Mrs Whiteleg,
Please to give us an Easter egg
If you won't give us an Easter egg,
Your hens will lay all coddled eggs,
An' your cocks lay all stones.

In the 19th century, it was common at Easter for poorer people, often children, to go from door to door to beg for food. Sometimes they sing chants in the hope of securing more donations.

Theobromine

The chemical in chocolate that makes it incredibly toxic to the Easter Bunny, other rabbits, and most pets, including cats and dogs.

The darker the chocolate found in a child's Easter basket, the higher the risk of toxicity.

Do not feed chocolate to the Easter Bunny no matter how much he/she asks!

"The great gift of Easter is hope."

Cardinal Basil Hume
Archbishop of Westminster, 1988